IN FELT TREELING

ACKNOWLEDGEMENTS //

Some sections of *IN FELT TREELING* were published previously in the magazine *580 Split;* others appeared as a chapbook bearing the same name, published by Soft Press.

The author wishes to thank his many friends, colleagues, and mentors (in this case, one in the same), especially Cynthia Sailers, Julian Brolaski, Trevor Calvert, Eli Drabman, Stephen Ratcliffe, and Elizabeth Willis (for their early and careful readings of this work as it was drafted in Oakland, California), and Thom Donovan, Kyle Schlesinger, Zack Finch, Andrew Rippeon, Rich Owens, Myung Mi Kim, Susan Howe, and Katja Geldhof (for their example, camaraderie, and advice as it was prepared for press in Buffalo, New York).

Cover Image and Details: *Dead Leaf 2*, Ryoko Aoki
(ink on paper, 11" x 8", 2003)

ISBN 978 092590 75 1

CHAX PRESS
411 North Seventh Avenue
Tucson, Arizona 85705

IN FELT TREELING

A LIBRETTO BY
MICHAEL CROSS

CHAX

IN FELT TREELING

Dramatis Personae

Lavinia (mezzo-soprano)
Eumenides (choral voice)
Forest (narrator)

(musk and tethered plumes
the treeless mouths
solemnity the very trouble
of direction
serving care by leaping from the
watch, assemblage such
cicadas warm the air
in threnody
a clime in thick

e.

as if to say / and when to spell it out
to distill / our pleasure
like baseness / how we talked of danger
stunned / in the wet covers

1.

our garments / just so
the darkness / a tumult
of many-runged / havens
the pleasure / left
burden / droves
snuffed / sensations wholly
used / wholly thin
how I freely / huff

(some variegated
cant for rolling
subject to gently
lash
the wantonness
of noon
incumbent
paper of the night
in softly
drop

1.

languish on the floor / makes me
curled / stretching toward the cave
roof where hang / the roses
where happily / and where

(come flora err
silhouette
dryness
of the clouds
to breathe

e.
what was called slate / rose
slack / rose-limbed
less liminal / consent
was necessary /

1.

brittle / I alert
though proclivity / no music
how natural / my tenacity, my cunning
suddenness / though too properly
suffer / herr ditch
my conqueror / I am a debutante
through / and through

(afeared dot
in yellow
wears at work
the river slips
to scoop
the ductal
mouth
all whet

e.
sallow blossom / dis-
sympathy your eyes / sort of
emphatic squints / spatially met
useless near you rend / already
yield / for instress

1.
I've thought / open little sequins
and have a model / with suctions
so forget it / nothing like wrists
against the air / the people
had a silhouette / for showing buildings
where they lived together / with hands
            / saying stop
when they had to / stop

(petals to the ground
the privy gown
fresh meted
welts
cruel fate

e.

a smith / wrought burlesque
handsome and to yield / and yield alike
forthright / cede
thy static / chatter there
a useless slag / of villainy

1.

in truth the fly hath / barbarous deft
leveled one, smashed / tyranny
saddle hinge / given
propensity / for trilling
given heat / pasties
treason at the head / of the lesion

(beneath the sycamore
drew crystal to the wood
spun iron lungs
affixed
the trees breathe shade
lisp addled haling
open mouth, o wisp

e.

wrought / a lithe wood
drawn / the light sank
there / applied the makeup
made a surface dent /

l.

the remnants of which / lust came off so
we didn't speak / the mouth cracked
what it meant / moving and soft sounded
ribbons / our compost tongue
pressed flat / against my side
the wine / out gilded age

(dress unloosened only fog
nettles yet
only little minded
truly had in bottom
of water
of walking there alone

(too yield
let touching smart
regards the lips
in acre felt
so listless
in their tears
unfettered
eyes in long
held lock

1.

my gown had little / white
was creamy tones / red like
a garden / was suddenly suspect
to assign such scene / were to sit
with mouths / how they came
bitter / in careful rows

(threads left hover
some in song
disdain the wood
a darker mouth
though wool spate
lop their wings
a threaded ave
flight against the throat

1.

trim / the dress left
there I stood / there
speechless / an ellipse of tin
worlds / is no place
to hunt / is hulking
left me no tone / the mood
stung vast / remove
to pieces / loitering the field

(tender-hefted thrush
already ornament
alack
driven mad
the starlight
dark

1.

met a cutting lisp / I trow
intent on vim / latent vestibule
I was / unkempt, I was
parable in lesson / consistent
with the dappled skylight / and glib
forms in will / to spite

e.

at the limbs / of osiris
as they tremble loose / they even
tassels / further coital
amusements / they took liberties
at first / of liberty a tender
and sore age / louse at work
the trouser hold / his sire
meant evasive pressure / pouring forth

l.

      / a lite venom
kiss / to do so wet

e.

                / the perforated
glide / scene such
cut / the heat
was difficult / to write about
the torso / the golden
trow for /

l.

my shallow eyes / perch
as for the wind / has limits
I am a vision / of chastity
            / to be won

(the very ground
a swallow
and of ground dolorous
song a bay forth
mouths in ternary
at list against
the willowed eave

(bonnets from the light
the fabric trees
no shade
hoved trimmings by
in wake
and trammeled
by the walk
the gyre
wake they're culling
baskets of the grass

1.

if length be illness / arms
may meager shine / though short
of patient / miniature
the sequined / near my wetted talk
I sat and watched / the ship pull close
a job for me / may
cleft / a song
wasp / weep

(an ardor
sunned there fabric grass
as sunned the whole tree
could sunder sheaves
a body littered knit

e.

            / have molted
ethos / though a girl

                / guard us
we are newly / blind

1.

as sparrow / as lone branch
as omen / dangled from the gash
with time / hideous
leverage / we have fable
we here moral / err
and dance against / the clad precipice

e.

clung / met opulent and downtrodden
the boys smelt loose / molten round
the soft / feathered lungs
some liquid made of them / a derelict
tender substitutes for men / and love

(in ribbons
cusped
the breeze
come opt
minutia
flush wash
tips should
slow lipped
sun glazed
glass in harm

1.

how they missed / my song
beneath its curt / draft
with rose lips / with lips otherwise
scentless / patterned against
the canvas / of my breast
for I am seaward / I sacrifice my poles
a current / lisp this useless

e.

to track her near / the wood
and raked / subordinate
grace / as smooth
the heat / its precious
wind / their fingers
serve impartial / sweep
                    / o tantrum
cyclic neath / you wooden lands

1.
I still / my hologram
and sheen skin / its caustic
shining / I am miniature
in sun / covered in little
bulbs / a moment
on this bed / of leaves
we are outside / the warmed dark
inside my thighs / is warmth

(singular held
in that ground
a feathered net
and land the mobile
let in lettered sieve

(desiccate too tied yield
a tint in berths
the upper wealth enlaced
a sanction
vines the more still
virus in the grass

e.

sprig and winter / deemed filament
caught blood / in deep buckets
and we were laughing / from the floor
we have two arms / each
we have / but two

(withdrew
back the whittled end
pageantry and willows
loosely knit
leaves dappled
sores new dim

1.

                / indiscriminant
at port / I stood the forest
bunched my dress / to climb
a tree / the birds made vision
legs would rather fissure / in the silt
and let my thighs / abscond

(erratum, the fragrant
shade led plastic
slow to wit

sorry for her
way in metal lets

(the grass iron
dusk by fanning
birds of prey
and to the wood
ran through

e.
liminal / used such and
such hue / a trim led hem
hung first / attest our effort

e.

hath added water / to the sea
hath disengaged our sight / its teeming brink
and naught our watch / upon your lips
anon / kindly met and tempt
tempt such / purely sharp in fragrance
that we propelled / that those around can see

1.

not paper / nor brittle
in that stolid / posturing
in brandish crux /
so brackish / as to splendor
I, helpless / I am
within the chamber / of my mouth
of what became / a remedy
within that even / night

(tell
pray summer
in its width
the cant for rolling
were to rend
in coarse
were to mold it hard
the morrow
over

e.
seldom level / what near authority
may flux / my garrulous
fold / solemn
in that teeth / were splendid cut
and marveled / how they ate
perchance / pearl
newly shed / a luxury

l.
doth leave me / still
in still skin / less
such / yield

1.

my dexterity / utter such
latent / in the fold
the inside glass / minced
weather in its common / place
I am hung thin / the body
of a tree / my body
too plastic / surely I miss
dancing / the trees have a different look

COME FLORA ERR

solos for mezzo-soprano

Tree

Intrepid throat, deeply in my ears and cup
hold—leave me stump. Dripping gums in that
tomorrow, my heart.

Tree

Sound made the beach warm. I'd been sitting
near the beach. If I'd hands to help me knit the
cord. If a cord at hand could be strung and with it
time and with time's bullishness. The hum made
the greens plague around the swell is where it
started. The sky as fickle as the sound.

Tree

Until I find a stream to cool this heat. Until my
mark runs freely in the heat, I cannot see. This
confidence doth mar my further moralizing, and
so prod forth, I told my lonesome, prod. Our
haven has us in retreat to hide the callus hand, our
nettled hut, your war in the one and pet. How I
was touched ashen—made a flowering rush. Runs
dripping from said wrists and with it cheer.

Tree

The hand in the courtyard, the bird dropped
trinkets in my mouth. The platform, love, the
hand was a thing with five things.

Tree

We met at the station. We met in the metal field
to melt and laugh.

Tree

The nettled branches, the horses' hooves cracking
in half, matting my hair. If I'd better developed
my solipsism, my ashen leg and limp. In four, the
flowers, their ruthless taxonomy and ignorance
of fawning, which made us reconsider. The flat
window with the open light.

Tree

There was comfort in how, standing with my fingers, a pocket of warmth for warmth. When you talked, your jaw did so much work I knew to use my language.

Tree

My only guilt came in a song / I knew in breath
and tone / but failed lightly with my own hot
tongue.

Tree

Its feathered bunches—rent gold surface with
numbers at the ridge's edge. The fire of its purple
wings. It's a cloud. It's as big as my eyes and I am
a cloud. My mouth retreats in terror near the
forest edge—its sound the color of the words.

Its beak is round and plastic. It drags its hull
against my face as I lower myself in flames, for
I am a cloud, I am the shape of a large crow. It's
no secret where I hide myself and in what pursed
condition.

Tree

The massive space between us—the many folded
bodies there by the road, up and down the quiet
of the road. The contrition in my lungs when I
knew my final sound and how it lit to blend my
voice.

Michael Cross edited the anthology *Involuntary Vision: after Akira Kurosawa's Dreams* (Avenue B, 2003), a companion piece to the New Brutalism reading series he founded in Oakland in 2001. He publishes Atticus/Finch Chapbooks (www.atticusfinch.org), and is currently editing a volume of the collected George Oppen Memorial Lectures for the Poetry Center at San Francisco State University. He is pursuing a doctoral degree in the Poetics Program at SUNY Buffalo, where he studies, particularly, the work of Louis Zukofsky. *In Felt Treeling* is his first full-length collection.